Clara Lidström
and
Annakarin Nyberg

LET'S GARDEN

A Step by Step Introduction

Illustrations by Katy Kimbell & Li Söderberg
Translated by Viktoria Lindbäck

Let's Garden: A Step by Step Introduction
by Clara Lidström and Annakarin Nyberg
Translation from Swedish by Viktoria Lindbäck
Illustrations by Katy Kimbell and Li Söderberg

Published by Little Gestalten, Berlin 2015
ISBN: 978-3-89955-747-3

Typefaces: Consolas by Lucas de Groot; Mirabelle by Jessica McCarty;
Core Circus by Hyun-Seung Lee, Dae-Hoon Hahm, and Min-Joo Ham

Printed by Livonia Print, Riga. Made in Europe.

The Swedish original edition *Odla* was published by Rabén &
Sjögren, Sweden 2015. © Clara Lidström and Annakarin Nyberg
© for the English edition: Little Gestalten, an imprint of
Die Gestalten Verlag GmbH & Co. KG, Berlin 2015

For more information, please visit little.gestalten.com.

Bibliographic information published by the Deutsche Nationalbibliothek. The Deutsche Nationalbibliothek lists this publication in
the Deutsche Nationalbibliografie; detailed bibliographic data are
available online at http://dnb.d-nb.de.

This book was printed on paper certified by the FSC®.

FSC
www.fsc.org
MIX
Paper from
responsible sources
FSC® C002795

Table of Contents

Tips and a Few Tricks

This is a book for those who like everything
that grows and germinates. It contains a
ton of fun growing projects that you can take
on entirely on your own! LET'S GARDEN is not a
book for grown-ups. In fact, they should stay
away as much as possible until it is time to
use a sharp tool or do something else that
might require their help.

The growing tips and crafts in this book
are just suggestions-you will probably come up
with something even more fun. With some soil,
water, and seeds you can do plenty of
exciting things…

9

HEAD POTS

You can make these funny figures with edible hairing by drawing faces on pots and grow cress or sunflowers in them. If you grow grass you can even give them a haircut!

TAKE OUT:

pot

paint

paintbrushes

pencils

soil

seeds, like cress, sunflower, or grass

saucer to place under the pot

pencil

saucer

Paintbrushes

seeds

paint

soil

pot

Put your finger in the soil and pull it out again. If no soil sticks to your finger, it needs to be watered. If your finger is muddy, you can wait a couple of days before giving it water.

HERE'S HOW YOU DO IT:

30 minutes

1 Paint the pot in a color you like.
Let the paint dry for 30 minutes.

2 Use a pencil to draw a face on
the pot.

3 Trace the pencil with a paintbrush and
paint. Let the paint dry.

12

4 Fill the pot with soil and sprinkle seeds on top.

5 Place a saucer underneath the pot and place in a window with lots of light. Water the pot so the seeds become moist. Check on the pot every day. The soil must never dry out.

6 After a couple of days, you will see a couple of green leaves or small strands of grass which will eventually grow into green hair. If you sowed cress or sunflower seeds, you can now give the plant a haircut and put the cutoffs on your sandwich!

SUNFLOWER

Sunflowers can grow really tall. The world's tallest sunflower was planted by a Dutch man and grew over 7 meters tall. That is even taller than a house! How tall can your sunflower grow?

TAKE OUT:

- pot
- soil
- saucer to place underneath the pot
- sunflower seeds
- supporting stick
- twine

stick

sunflower seeds

soil

saucer

pot

twine

If you want your sunflower
to grow really tall, try
watering it with "gold water".
Mix 100 milliliters of pee with
900 milliliters of water.
Sunflowers really
like gold water.

HERE'S HOW YOU DO IT:

1 Take out a pot, fill it with soil, and place the pot on a saucer.

2 Plant a sunflower seed a couple of centimeters into the soil.

3 Water the pot properly and place it in a window.

4 A couple of weeks later, you will see a sprout. That's when you should place the pot in a light-filled but cool window.

5 When the sunflower has grown about a foot tall, it needs something to support it. Place a stick in the soil and use the twine to tie it together with the flower.
The taller the sunflower grows, the longer sticks you will need.

6 After about 8 weeks, the sunflower seed has grown into a nice plant.

With a lot of sun and some fertilizer the sunflower can grow really tall.

7 Move the flower to a bigger pot or plant it in your garden flowerbed. That will make it grow even taller. Don't forget to water it as soon as the soil feels dry.

BIRD FOOD

When your sunflower has bloomed, you can
save the seeds and plant new sunflowers next year.
Or you can use them to feed the birds.
Now we will show you how to do that!

pens

TAKE OUT:

twine

500 grams coconut fat

sauce pan

coffee mugs or
plastic cups

650 grams bird seeds
and different kinds
of nuts

knife

a pair of scissors

twine

pens

sauce pan

knife

nuts

coconut fat

bird seeds

a pair of scissors

coffee mugs

18

Do you know what a seed bomb is? Well, it's a small ball of soil and seeds that you can throw on to empty land and other boring places that need to be refreshed with flowers. Try making your own seed bomb sometime.

HERE'S HOW YOU DO IT:

1 Ask a grown-up for help with melting the coconut fat. Melt it at a low temperature so that the fat doesn't spray.

2 Pour the coconut fat into the cups.

3 Chop the nuts with a knife. Ask a grown-up for help.

4 Mix the nuts and seeds and pour them into the coconut fat.

5 Take out a pair of scissors and some twine. Cut the twine into a couple of pieces. They should be at least 30 centimeters long.

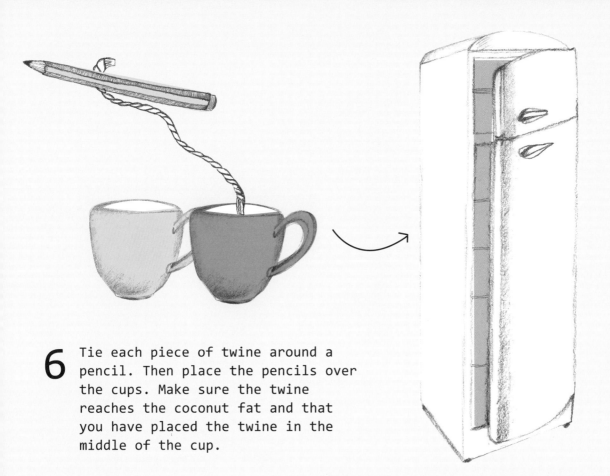

6 Tie each piece of twine around a pencil. Then place the pencils over the cups. Make sure the twine reaches the coconut fat and that you have placed the twine in the middle of the cup.

7 Refrigerate the bird food and let it sit for a couple of hours. Take the lumps out of the mugs and hang them in the trees. Invite the birds to the party!

apple Wreath

We also tried threading a couple of apples on a steel wire and hanging them in a tree. Birds like apples. Can you think of anything else to feed them with?

If you want, you can make a bean competition. Try placing different kinds of beans on top of wet cotton and see which one grows the quickest.

BEANS & BEAN GAMES

Beans grow very quickly and there are many different kinds to choose from. Wax beans, French beans, or beans with beautiful flowers! We used large white broad beans that we bought from the grocery store. We made a game out of the beans that were left over.

TAKE OUT:

twine

cotton

BEANS:

cotton

dried beans

pot or a mold to grow in

saucer to place
underneath the pot

soil

sticks

twine

pot

BEAN GAME / TIC-TAC-TOE:

a piece of a leftover
board or a piece of
cardboard

colored pens

dried beans

colored pens

dried beans

sticks

saucer

soil

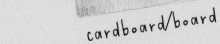
cardboard/board

HERE'S HOW YOU DO IT: BEANS

From above

1 Spread out cotton in a pot or a mold. Wet the cotton with water.

2 Place the beans on top of the cotton. Place a saucer underneath the pot and place it in a window with lots of light. It is important that the cotton doesn't dry out. You also shouldn't water it too much since that can spoil the beans and make them moldy.

3 Soon, the beans will grow little leaves and then it is time to move the beans to pots with soil. Don't forget to water them regularly. When the beanstalks have grown to become about 15 centimeters tall, they need support to lean against. Place a stick in the soil and carefully tie it to the plant using some twine.

4 As soon as the weather gets warmer outside and the soil is no longer cold, you should move the beans outside. If you don't have a garden or flowerbed, you can move the beans to bigger pots that contain more soil.

HERE'S HOW YOU DO IT:
BEAN GAME/TIC-TAC-TOE

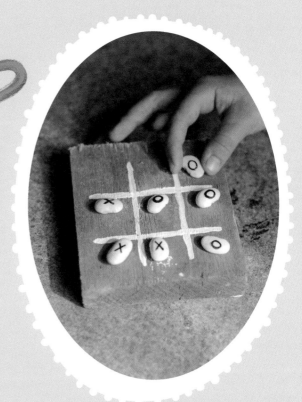

1 You need something solid on which you can draw the playing field. We used a piece of a sawed-off wooden board.
You can also cut out a piece of cardboard.

2 Draw 9 squares on the board or piece of cardboard.

You and your opponent alternate drawing Xs and Os on the board until someone has three in a row or all squares are filled.

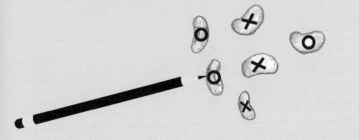

3 Pick out 6 white beans. Draw a big X on 3 of them and a big O on the other 3. Now it is time to find somebody to play with!

RABBIT POOP BEADS

Are you curious about what bunnies eat?
In that case you should try planting rabbit poop.
You know, those round, brown, dry beads that you can
find in the woods.

TAKE OUT:

hammer

1 nail

rabbit poop beads
metal or plastic box
1 nail
hammer
soil
saucer to place underneath
the pot

box

saucer

soil

rabbit poop beads

In the wintertime, rabbits change color from brown to white. Even artic foxes and ermines change into a winter white fur coat. That helps them hide better when it starts snowing.

HERE'S HOW YOU DO IT:

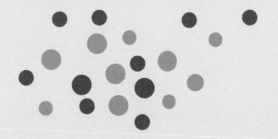

1 Grab a friend and go search for rabbit poop in the woods. You need about 20 beads.

2 Make a hole at the bottom of the box using a nail and a hammer. Ask a grown-up for help. The holes make sure water can escape in case the soil becomes too wet.

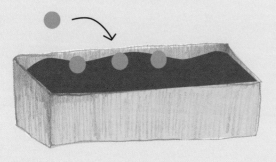

3 Fill the box with soil. Press the beads a couple of centimeters apart into the soil.

4 Carefully cover the beads with soil, place a saucer underneath the pot, and add lots of water. Finish by washing your hands thoroughly.

We planted lots of rabbit poop and really all sorts of different things started to grow! What did your rabbit eat?

5 Place the pot in a window with lots of light. All plants need sunlight. That simply makes them grow a little bit quicker.

6 Don't forget to water it often. The soil should never dry out. Now wait and see what springs from the soil!

In the Fall when the geranium has finished blossoming, you can put it behind a curtain and water it less often. When Spring returns, you should put it back in a light spot, give it new soil, and add more water. That will make new leaves grow out!

GERANIUMS & WEEDS

Now you will learn how to make many different
geraniums from one single plant. Next to the geraniums
are a bundle of weeds waiting for a task.
You will soon see what that is!

TAKE OUT:

geranium

GERANIUM:

geranium

a pair of scissors

pot

soil

saucer to place underneath the pot

To make your own flower
pot, wrap a broad sheet of
newspaper around a glass.
Fold the extra ends into
the glass, and fill it with
soil. Done!

WEEDS:

weeds

pot

soil

saucer to
place underneath the pot

a pair of scissors

pot

pot

saucer

soil

weeds

HERE'S HOW YOU DO IT: GERANIUM

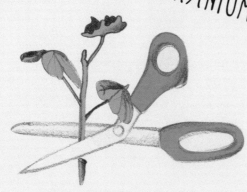

1 Cut off a shoot from the geranium plant. Fill a pot with soil and plant the shoot 3-4 centimeters into the soil. Make sure the shoot is standing steadily.

2 Place a saucer underneath the pot, add water, and place it in a window with lots of light. It's important that the soil doesn't dry out.

3 In a couple of weeks it is time to replant the flower in a bigger pot and give it more soil.

4 When there is no longer frost outside and the days are starting to become warmer, you can move your geranium outside. With time, it will start to grow white, red, or pink flowers!

HERE'S HOW YOU DO IT: WEEDS

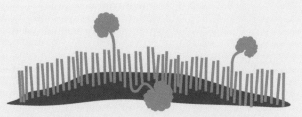

1 Check your lawn for tiny, tiny leaves that look like the picture. Carefully lift them from the ground using your hands and make sure you get as much of the roots as possible.

2 Place the plant along with other flowers or by itself in a pot with soil. Water it carefully and place the pot in a light spot. Place a saucer underneath the pot.

3 This weed is called ground ivy and it grows super-fast! It is also very durable. We like that! That makes growing it simple, cheap, and fun.

Do you know another type of weed that can be used for something?

GARLIC & CHEESE

We had some left-over garlic cloves in our refrigerator that had started to grow small green and yellow shoots. Instead of using them for cooking we tried placing them in a pot. From the plant we made a type of cream cheese. Yummy!

TAKE OUT:

GARLIC:

kitchen towels

saucer

cloves of garlic

pot

soil

saucer to place underneath the pot

CHEESE:

300 grams sour cream,
soured milk,
or yoghurt (plain)

coffee filter and
something to hold it

bowl

garlic leaves

a pair of scissors

salt

pepper

pot

cloves of garlic

saucer

kitchen towels

plate

soil

bowl

salt

pepper

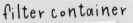
a pair of scissors

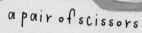
sour cream

garlic leaves

coffee filter

filter container

We used garlic for our cheese but you can just as well add other things you like such as cress or chives. What would you like to flavor your cheese with?

HERE'S HOW YOU DO IT: GARLIC

1 Wet a couple of kitchen towels and place them on a small plate. Place the cloves of garlic on the towels and place the plate in a window with lots of light. In a couple of days the cloves will have developed roots.

2 Take out a pot and fill it with soil. Plant the cloves of garlic about 2 centimeters into the soil with the pointy side facing up and cover them with dirt.

3 Place a saucer underneath the pot and place it in a window with lots of light. In about 1 week the cloves will have started to produce tiny, slim, green leaves.

You can support the plants with sticks.

4 When the plants have grown about 15 centimeters, you can cut off a couple of leaves. Cut them into small pieces and sprinkle them over a salad or make your own garlic cream cheese. It's simple to do and tastes delicious on a sandwich!

HERE'S HOW YOU DO IT:

CHEESE

1 Strain the sour cream through a coffee filter. Place the container with the filter on top of a bowl and put it in the refrigerator for until the next few days.

2 Pour out the fluid that has gathered in the bowl and replace it with the sour cream which has become a thick cream.

3 Grab a pair of scissors and cut a few garlic leaves into the bowl. Cut tiny, tiny pieces. Add salt and pepper. Stir carefully.

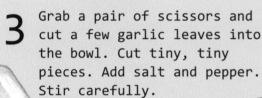

4 Your cheese is now ready, and it's time to spread it on a sandwich and taste it!

POTATOES IN A BUCKET

Have you ever thought about the fact that you can grow your own food? Potatoes actually grow really well in a bucket on the balcony. Plant them in the spring and eat them in the late summer. Delicious! The potatoes grow as long as the stalk is green. That means you can choose how big you want your potatoes to be!

TAKE OUT:

hammer

1 nail

bucket that can contain about 10 liters

gravel

soil

3-5 potatoes

gravel

bucket

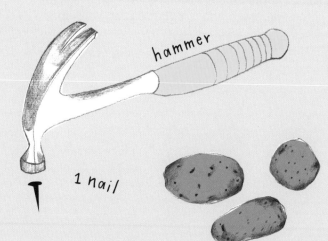
hammer

1 nail

soil

potatoes

How are the plants going to survive when you leave the house? Start by watering the pot really well. Then take out an empty plastic bottle and make a tiny hole in the cap. Fill the bottle with water. Screw on the cap, turn the bottle upside down, and push it into the soil. Done!

1 Use a hammer and nail to make a hole in the bottom of the bucket. Ask a grownup for help. The hole lets the water out in case the soil gets too wet.

15 cm

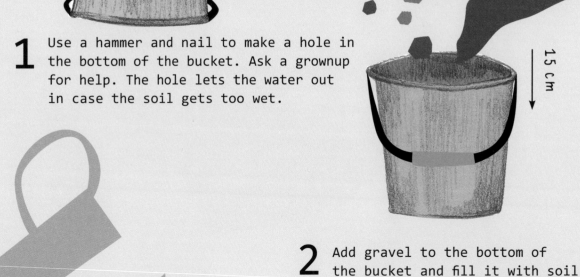

2 Add gravel to the bottom of the bucket and fill it with soil. Then place the potatoes about 15 centimeters into the soil.

3 Place the bucket outside and water it until it's really wet. Now you just have to have patience. The soil must not dry out so check if you need to water it daily.

4 After a couple of weeks, the potato haulm will start to appear from the soil. Place the bucket in a sunny and light spot.

5 When the haulm has grown about 10 centimeters, the soil is supposed to be piled. That means you take the soil and form a pile at the root of the haulm.

It's important to pile the soil around the haulm. Otherwise the sun will make it green and poisonous.

6 After about 2 months, the potatoes are ready to be harvested. Carefully put your hands in the ground and see if you can find any potatoes.

TOMATOES & NAME ROCKS

Growing your own tomatoes is really fun! But they are quite thirsty so don't forget to water them. Tomatoes also need a lot of light. That's why it's best to plant them in the early spring.

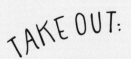 TAKE OUT:

rocks

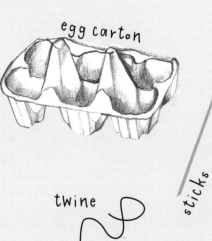 egg carton

TOMATOES:

egg carton

soil

tomato seeds

pots

sticks

twine

saucer to place underneath the pots

sticks

twine

 sharpie

NAME ROCKS:

rocks

paint

brushes

sharpies (waterproof)

varnish

brushes

paint

HOBBYPAINT

varnish

soil

saucer

pots

VARNISH

tomato seeds

HERE'S HOW YOU DO IT: TOMATOES

1 Fill the holes in the carton with soil. Plant a tomato seed in each hole. Place the carton in a window with lots of light and water it regularly.

2 After a couple of weeks, the seed will have started to grow. Place the carton in your sunniest window and water it regularly. The soil must never dry out.

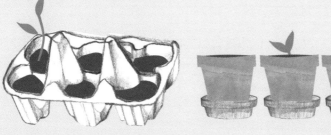

3 When the shoots have grown its first pair of leaves, each shoot should be replanted in a bigger pot. Plant the shoot deep enough for the soil to reach the first pair of leaves. Place the plants in a sunny but cool area. Place a saucer underneath the pots.

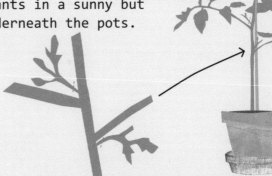

4 Place a stick in the pot as support for the plant while it grows. Tie the stick and plant together using some twine. Let the soil dry between watering it.

5 The plant will keep growing side shoots. You should cut these off because it helps the plant grow actual tomatoes. The plant will soon blossom and it's those flowers that eventually turn into tomatoes.

HERE'S HOW YOU DO IT: NAME ROCKS

1 Pick out a couple of nice, smooth rocks from nature.

2 Paint the rocks in different colors. Let the paint dry for 30 minutes.

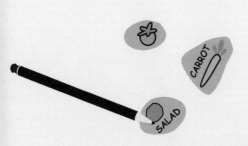

3 Write the names of the plants with a sharpie.

4 Finish the rocks by adding a coat of varnish. Let the varnish dry before you place the name rocks in the pots.

black currants

calendular

plantain

nettles

marigold

sorrel

hops

NATURE'S PANTRY

There are plenty of things you can eat in nature. We are going to show you a couple of examples. Ask a grown-up to check if it's an edible plant before you taste it!

You can make nettle soup from nettles.

nettles

Nettles will burn you so be careful when you pick them. Protect your hands with garden gloves or a pair of plastic bags.

Sorrels are delicious in a salad or on their own.

To make a simple vegetable soup special just add a handful of nettles and heavy cream and puree everything.

sorrels

Hops are climbing plants that develope tiny light green pine cones at the end of the summer. You can make tea from the pine cones. You can also make tea from black currant leaves.

hops

black currants

Start by drying hops pine cones and black currant leaves. You can do this by spreading them out on a paper tissue. After a couple of weeks, they are dry enough to be used for tea.

Take 3 dry hops pine cones and place them in a cup. Ask a grown-up to help you boil water and add it to the cup. Let it simmer for 10 minutes. Remove the pine cones or leaves with a spoon. Be careful when you taste it to make sure you don't burn your tongue. Which tea do you prefer?

Plantain is a weed that often grows in lawns. In the past it was used as band aids since many people thought it helped heal wounds more quickly.

Marigold and calendular are two common flowers in our summer gardens.

plantain

marigold

These flowers are edible. Cut off the leaves and sprinkle them over a salad to make it really colorful. You can also try eating them on their own. What do you think of the flavor?

calendular

Do you want to try chewing resin? Look for pine resin that has solidified. Break off a piece and carefully chew it. At first it is hard and crumbly. After a while it becomes soft, just like chewing gum.

Epilogue for Grown-ups

The inspiration for LET'S GARDEN came from our own
children and their fascination with everything
that grows and thrives. This book demonstrates
how to cultivate plants that are both edible and
beautiful. We also grow things that are a little
bit silly, like planting rabbit poop or making
funny hairdos of fast-growing grass.

We also want to inspire kids to consider nature
as a pantry. What grows in our proximity that
we can taste? We also provide tips on what you can
do with the stuff you have grown: for example,
the sunflower can become bird food and the garlic
can flavor a homemade cream cheese.

Step by step and with the help of the illustrations, tiny growers are guided through the
projects. Our ambition is that grown-ups should
be almost superfluous. You don't need any advanced
tools or expensive materials in order to follow
the descriptions. You also don't need access
to large growing areas. Our tips work just as well
with small window sills, balconies, or flowerbeds.
It's simply a book for everybody!

Annakarin & Clara